SPACE FIRSTS™

YURI GAGARIN
The First Man in Space

Heather Feldman

The Rosen Publishing Group's
PowerKids Press™

For my Dad, Sy Wane, my mentor, my protector, my inspiration.
You are a kind, wise, gentle soul, and you are loved more than words can say.

Published in 2003 by The Rosen Publishing Group, Inc.
29 East 21st Street, New York, NY 10010

First Edition

Editor: Nancy MacDonell Smith
Book Design: Mike Donnellan

Photo Credits: Cover © Rykoff Collection/CORBIS; pp. 4, 8, 12, 16, 20 (inset) © Bettmann/CORBIS; p. 15 © Roger Ressmeyer/COR-BIS; pp. 7, 11, 19, 20 Courtesy of the private collection of Alla Pavlova.

Feldman, Heather.
Yuri Gagarin : the first man in space / by Heather Feldman.— 1st ed.
    p. cm. — (Space firsts)
Includes bibliographical references and index.
ISBN 0-8239-6245-8 (lib. bdg.)
1. Gagarin, Yuri Alekseyevich, 1934–1968—Juvenile literature. 2. Astronauts—Russia—Biography—Juvenile literature. 3. Astronauts—Soviet Union—Biography—Juvenile literature. [1. Gagarin, Yuri Alekseyevich, 1934–1968. 2. Astronauts.] I. Title.
TL789.85.G3 F45 2003
629.45'0092—dc21

                        2001006027

Manufactured in the United States of America

Contents

Gagarin's Early Life

Yuri Gagarin was born on March 9, 1934, near the town of Gzhatsk, Russia. Russia was called the Soviet Union at that time. Gagarin's parents worked on a farm. His father was a carpenter, and his mother worked as a dairymaid. Gagarin was the third of four children. He often helped his parents with their work on the farm. Gagarin's favorite subjects in school were science and math.

Gagarin studied to be a metalworker. In 1955, Gagarin decided to join a local flying club. His path in life was about to change forever.

This photograph of Yuri Gagarin, fighter pilot and space pioneer, was taken the year he blasted into space. Gagarin was 27 years old at the time.

Flying High

After joining the Saratov Flying Club in 1955, Yuri Gagarin learned quickly and became a very skilled flier. That same year Gagarin made his first **parachute** jump from an airplane. Although he was frozen with fear at first, Gagarin made the jump. From the moment he joined the Saratov Flying Club, Gagarin dreamed of flying airplanes. Yuri Gagarin studied hard and graduated from a top flying school in 1957. He then joined the Soviet Air Force. At the same time, the Soviet Union **launched** the first human-made **satellites** into space. Gagarin married a nursing student named Valentina Goryacheva. Gagarin and his wife had two children. He spent the next two years as a fighter pilot.

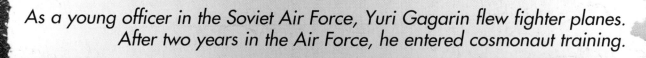

As a young officer in the Soviet Air Force, Yuri Gagarin flew fighter planes. After two years in the Air Force, he entered cosmonaut training.

Vostok 1

rockets

In Russia astronauts are called **cosmonauts**. In 1959, Yuri Gagarin asked to be considered for cosmonaut training. Thousands of other pilots wanted the same thing. Gagarin was selected in the first group of pilots and began weeks of physical testing. Gagarin passed the tests. In 1960, he became 1 of 12 pilots accepted into the difficult training program. Gagarin and the other pilots learned about space **navigation**, rockets, **astronomy**, and the **atmosphere**. They were trained to handle the dangers of spaceflight. Gagarin liked spending time in the model of *Vostok 1*, the spaceship that would one day **orbit** Earth. He had no idea that he'd be the man inside the real thing! After only nine months of training, the cosmonauts were told that *Vostok 1* would launch on April 12, 1961.

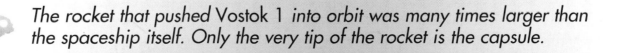

The rocket that pushed Vostok 1 *into orbit was many times larger than the spaceship itself. Only the very tip of the rocket is the capsule.*

The Chief Designer

The man in charge of the Soviet space program was named Sergei Korolev. At that time, the Soviets were keeping everything about their space program a secret. No one in America knew Korolev's name. He became known to the outside world as the Chief Designer. Korolev made sure his cosmonauts were ready for the **challenge** of spaceflight. To make sure they were strong and healthy, he had them run long distances and do gymnastics. The cosmonauts practiced their jumping and landing. Korolev even locked them in a dark, silent room for days. He put them in a machine that spun them around and shook them up. The cosmonauts were **exposed** to very hot temperatures and very cold ones. Korolev wanted the cosmonauts to be prepared for anything that might happen on the **incredible** journey into space.

Gherman Titov was one of the cosmonauts who trained with Yuri Gagarin. When this photo of him was taken, it was still not decided who would be the first cosmonaut to travel to space.

The Chief Designer Makes His Pick

Sergei Korolev knew the first cosmonaut chosen to go into space must be someone who could survive a rocket launch, **zero gravity**, and the reentry into Earth's atmosphere. Korolev asked the cosmonauts to choose the person they felt would be the best one to make the journey into space. Most of the cosmonauts chose Gagarin. Korolev chose Gagarin, too. Yuri Gagarin was strong and physically fit. He was up for the challenge.

The night before the launch, Korolev crept into Gagarin's bedroom to make sure his cosmonaut was sleeping soundly. After a good night's sleep, Yuri Gagarin awoke on the morning of April 12, 1961. It was the morning of the launch. Gagarin was eager and excited. Soon he would surprise the world.

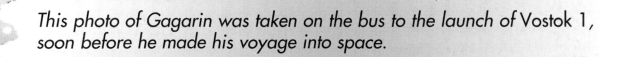

This photo of Gagarin was taken on the bus to the launch of Vostok 1, *soon before he made his voyage into space.*

13

Blast Off!

Yuri Gagarin began his journey into space at 9:07 A.M., Moscow time. A few hours earlier, Gagarin had been awakened so that his blood pressure and heart rate could be checked. He was ready for his flight. Gagarin arrived at his spacecraft at 7:30 A.M. He waited for an hour and a half, and then the countdown began. As Gagarin heard a loud roar and felt his rocket shake, he yelled, "*Poyekhali!*" which means "Let's go!" in Russian. Within minutes Yuri Gagarin was in space. The *Vostok 1* rocket traveled at a speed of between 17,000 and 18,000 miles per hour (27,359–28,968 km/h)! It took Gagarin in a path around Earth at 203 miles (327 km) above the ground. This path is called the orbit. Gagarin was in a place no human had ever been in before.

The interior of Vostok 1 was about the size of the inside of a small car. Gagarin did not have much room to move during his flight.

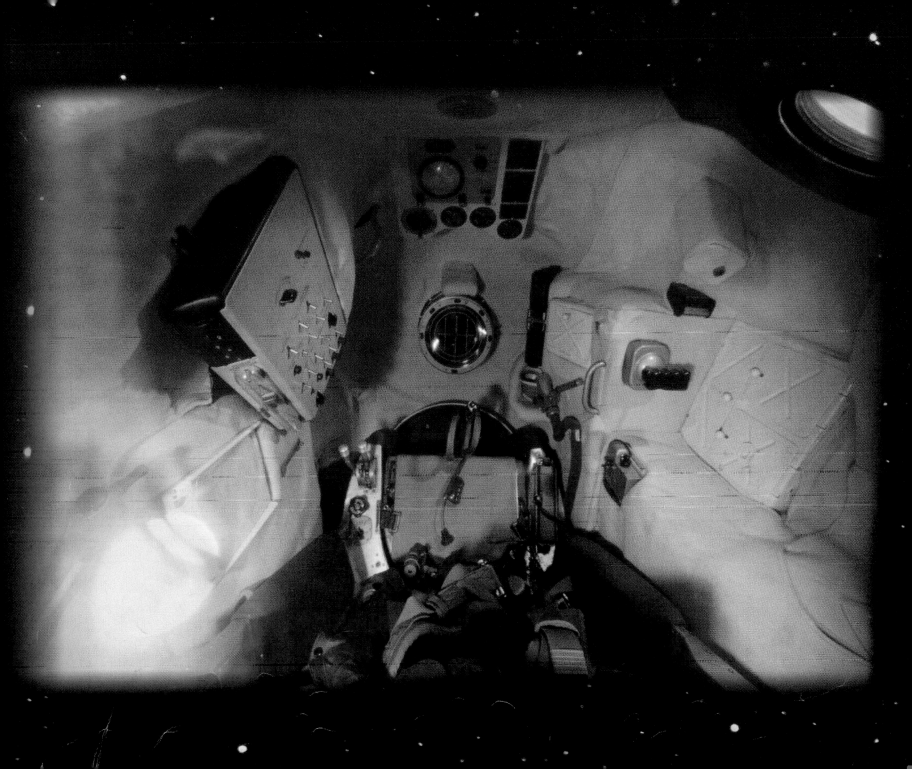

Gagarin In Space

During the spaceflight, Gagarin had no control over the rocket. Everything was controlled by scientists on the ground. Gagarin spent his time recording what he saw and how he felt in a log book. When he let go of his pencil and book, they floated around the capsule! They were weightless in space because there was no **gravity** to hold them down. Gagarin noticed that drops of water floated around, too. He reported, "Weightlessness does not feel unpleasant. Am feeling fine." Gagarin looked out of his capsule and saw a most magnificent sight, the planet Earth. Gagarin said, "It is **unique** and beautiful." After 78 minutes in space, Gagarin was about to finish his incredible journey. It was time to return home.

After Vostok 1 *returned to Earth, many people wanted to see it. This photo was taken in Tokyo, where* Vostok 1 *was on display.*

Returning to Earth

The dangerous part of Yuri Gagarin's mission was just beginning. When Gagarin passed over Africa, the **retro-rockets** fired. *Vostok 1* slowed down and started to reenter Earth's atmosphere. As it traveled through the atmosphere, the outside of the capsule became extremely hot. Gagarin noticed it was so hot that it glowed red. Luckily the temperature didn't change inside the capsule. Then something happened that the Soviet Union kept a secret for many years. At about 23,000 feet (7,010 m) above ground, the capsule hatch flew off. Gagarin **ejected** himself from the capsule and began to float down with a parachute. The rocket floated down with a separate parachute. Gagarin landed at 10:55 A.M. Moscow time. His voyage to space lasted for 108 minutes. The adventure would be remembered forever.

Top: *From left to right, cosmonauts Yuri Gagarin, Pavel Popovich, Gherman Titov, and Andrian Nikolayev.* Bottom: *Two days after his return to Earth, Gagarin gave a report to high-ranking Soviet officials.*

International Hero

Yuri Gagarin was an instant hero. People around the world knew about his accomplishment and wanted to meet him. The Soviets awarded him many honors.

At the same time Gagarin became famous around the world, Sergei Korolev wanted to hide the fact that Gagarin had landed by parachute, without his spacecraft. Korolev knew that international rules stated a pilot must stay in his craft from takeoff to landing for his flight to count as a real flight. Because Gagarin had to eject early, Korolev worried that Gagarin might not get credit for being the first man in space. Many years later the truth came out, but no one would ever **discount** the incredible flight taken by Yuri Gagarin.

Yuri Gagarin speaks at Dynamo Stadium in Briansk, a town near Moscow, on May 26, 1966. Everyone wanted to see the first man in space.

The Vostok 1 Mission and Beyond

April 12, 1961 is a day in history that will never be forgotten. This mission marked the beginning of many more amazing journeys to space. It helped push America to strengthen its space program. President John F. Kennedy promised Americans that "before the decade is out" humans would set foot on the moon. Sadly, neither the president nor Yuri Gagarin lived to see that day. Gagarin always wanted to return to space. During a routine test flight in 1968, his jet crashed. Yuri Gagarin's incredible life had come to an end. When American astronauts Neil Armstrong and Edwin Aldrin Jr. landed on the moon, they left one of Yuri Gagarin's medals there. This was a fitting **tribute** to the first man in space.

Glossary

astronomy (uh-STRAH-nuh-mee) The science of the Sun, Moon, planets, and stars.

atmosphere (AT-muh-sfeer) The layer of gases that surrounds an object in space. On Earth, this layer is air.

challenge (CHA-lenj) A difficulty in an undertaking that is stimulating.

cosmonauts (KOZ-muh-nots) The Russian word for astronauts.

discount (dis-KOWNT) To disregard or minimize.

ejected (ee-JEKT-ed) To be driven or thrown out from within.

exposed (ik-SPOHZD) Open to the air.

gravity (GRA-vih-tee) The natural force that causes objects to move or tend to move toward the center of Earth.

incredible (in-KRED-ih-bul) Hard or impossible to believe.

launched (LAWNCHD) Pushed a spacecraft into the air.

navigation (na-vuh-GAY-shun) A way of figuring out which way a spaceship will move.

orbit (OR-bit) The circular path traveled by one body around another body in space.

parachute (PAYR-uh-shoot) A large device of fabric, similar to an umbrella, that opens in midair and allows a person or an object to descend at a safe rate of speed, as from an airplane.

retro-rockets (REH-troh-rah-kits) Engines that are fired to bring a spacecraft back to Earth.

satellites (SA-til-eyets) Human-made or natural objects that orbit another body.

tribute (tri-BYUT) Something done or given to show thanks or respect.

unique (yoo-NEEK) One of a kind.

zero gravity (ZEE-roh GRA-vih-tee) Weightlessness.

Index

Web Sites

Due to the changing nature of Internet links, PowerKids Press has developed an online list of Web sites related to the subject of this book. This site is updated regularly. Please use this link to access the list:

www.powerkidslinks.com/sf/gagarin/